THE
GREAT
PHILOSOPHERS

Consulting Editors
Ray Monk and Frederic Raphael

D1313282

ACKNOWLEDGEMENTS

The author and publishers wish to thank the following for permission to use copyright material:

Oxford University Press for material from David Hume, *Treatise of Human Nature*, ed. L A Selby-Bigge, revised by P H Nidditch, 2nd ed. (1998); David Hume, *Enquiries concerning Human Understanding and concerning the Principles of Morals*, ed. L A Selby-Bigge, revised by P H Nidditch, 3rd ed. (1975); David Hume, *Essays* (1963); David Hume, *The Natural History of Religion*, ed. A Wayne Colver and J V Price (1976); and David Hume, *Dialogues concerning Natural Religion*, ed. Norman Kemp Smith (1935).

Every effort has been made to trace the copyright holders but if any have been inadvertently overlooked the publishers will be pleased to make the necessary arrangement at the first opportunity.

Anthony Quinton

HUME

PHŒNIX

To Leon and Shelby

A PHOENIX PAPERBACK

First published in Great Britain in 1998 by
Phoenix, a division of the Orion Publishing Group Ltd
Orion House
5 Upper Saint Martin's Lane
London, WC2H 9EA

A catalogue reference is available
from the British Library

ISBN 0 753 80186 8

Typeset by Deltatype Ltd, Birkenhead, Merseyside

Printed in Great Britain by
Clays Ltd, St Ives plc

HUME

Anthony Quinton

ABBREVIATIONS FOR HUME'S WORKS

E = *Enquiries: concerning the human understanding and concerning the principles of morals*, ed. L. A. Selby-Bigge. 2nd edn, Oxford, 1902.

D = *Dialogues concerning natural religion*, ed. Norman Kemp Smith, Oxford, 1935.

Ess = *Essays*, Oxford, 1963.

N = *The Natural History of Religion and Dialogues Concerning Natural Religion*, ed. A. W. Glyn and J. V. Price, Oxford, 1976.

T = *Treatise of Human Nature*, ed. L. A. Selby-Bigge. Oxford, 1888 and later.

INTRODUCTION

Hume is the greatest of British philosophers: the most profound, penetrating and comprehensive. His work is the high point of the predominant empiricist tradition in British philosophy that begins with William of Ockham in the fourteenth century and runs through Bacon and Hobbes, Locke and Berkeley, continues, after Hume, with Bentham and J.S. Mill and culminates in the analytic philosophy of the present century, which was inaugurated by Bertrand Russell and is still posthumously presided over by him.

He was neither as sensible nor, partly for that reason, as influential a philosopher as Locke. Where Locke recommended an attitude of caution or reserve in belief that was welcome to many after a century of horrible religious conflict, Hume seemed to deal in paradoxes, to end up in a total scepticism which could be relieved only by frivolity. Locke's political doctrines contributed to some extent, particularly through Voltaire's enthusiastic endorsement, to the thinking that inspired the French Revolution and played a much larger part in the design of the American Constitution. The utilitarians of the nineteenth century made a simplified version of Hume's moral and political theory effective, as the basis of a radical variety of liberalism of which he would hardly have approved. Until the twentieth century, the main effect of his theoretical philosophy was negative, provoking a number of philosophers to address themselves to the business of refuting him. Kant said that Hume had 'woken him from his dogmatic slumber'. Thomas Reid, the Scottish common-sense philosopher, saw Hume as having brilliantly demonstrated the implicit absurdity of the Lockian 'theory of ideas'. T.H. Green wrote an enormous introduction to an edition of Hume's works, pursuing his supposed mistakes with unwavering resolve. Only in the twentieth century has he been acknowledged as an important constructive philosopher.

Hume was profoundly Scottish, by birth, preferred residence, loyalty, accent and mannerisms. He was the most distinguished luminary of the Scottish Enlightenment of the eighteenth century, which also included Adam Smith, the great economist, Adam Ferguson, the founder of sociology, the historian William Robertson and many others. They made up a wonderfully lively and stimulating intellectual environment in which all the human sciences were pursued: philosophy, history, politics, economics, criticism and the non-dogmatic study of religion. The style of these eighteenth-century Scots compares very favourably, in its rigour and generality, with the more easy-going, literary mode of thought of their English contemporaries. (There is the exception of Samuel Johnson, but he might have benefited from a bit of system and from less watery people to dispute with.)

Hume shared with his associates, and, indeed, most philosophers of his epoch, two qualities that distinguish him and them from philosophers of the present day. In the first place, his scope of interests was extraordinarily wide. He did not just write about but made contributions of serious importance to theoretical and moral philosophy, political theory, economics and the study of religion, historical and doctrinal, writing memorably about miracles, the freedom of the will, the immortality of the soul and suicide, as well as devastating the kind of rational or natural religion, the deism, which was as far as most Enlightenment thinkers thought it practically or theoretically reasonable to go.

But he was far better known in his own time as a historian, and far better rewarded for it. His youthful philosophical masterpiece, the *Treatise on Human Nature*, if it did not, as he gloomily proclaimed, 'fall dead-born from the press', did not sell out its small first edition for several decades. His later six-volume *History of England* was a bestseller.

The other quality distinguishing Hume professionally from contemporary philosophers is the literary character of his ambitions. In his brief *Autobiography* he refers to 'my ruling passion, my love of literary fame'. He was a conscious, elegant writer of an Augustan type, producing courtly, balanced sentences, coloured by concrete analogies and examples. Samuel Johnson said, 'Why, Sir, his style is not English. The structure of his sentences is French.' That is not self-evidently a fault. Hume wrote the *Treatise* during a long stay in France and it may be that work which Johnson had in mind. Philosophy in the eighteenth century was part of polite literature; in the universities it was only a timid adjunct of theology and classical studies. Hume was addressing generally educated readers, not academics, who on the whole have never liked him. He is, indeed, a careless writer, too easy-going to bother about loose ends. More to the point stylistically, he was a good deal inferior to the more or less perfect Berkeley, but that is hardly a weakness and it is hard to think of any British philosopher after him who wrote as well as he did, with the possible exception of F.H. Bradley.

There is one important limitation to Hume's intellectual equipment. Marvellously knowledgeable about the humanities, he seems to have known next to nothing about, and to have had no interest in, mathematics and natural science. That did not do too much harm. He wrote perfectly good, more or less Leibnizian, sense about mathematics. If he wrongly supposed all natural science to be causal, at least its elementary parts are. Where his mathematical weakness let him down is in part 2 of the *Treatise*, in which some very weird things are said about space and time. He says, for example, that an extended whole must be composed of unextended parts, which are nevertheless finite in number and equipped with such perceptible qualities as colour. Commentators almost universally draw a veil over this part of Hume's work.

LIFE

Hume was born in Edinburgh in 1711. His family came from, and mainly lived in, the Borders, at their Ninewells estate, which lay between Berwick to the east and Duns (where Duns Scotus may have been born, but was probably not) to the west. His father died when he was two, so his devoted, intensely Calvinistic mother was the main early influence. The family's home and religion would have made them deeply unsympathetic to the Jacobite attempt in 1715 to install the legitimate, Catholic monarch, who should have been James III, on the throne.

Hume went to Edinburgh University at the early age of twelve, quite usual at the time, and left three years later. He then turned unwillingly to the study of law, but gave most of his attention to Cicero and other classical authors. After some sort of nervous breakdown and a brief spell in a Bristol merchant's office, he retired for three years to rural France, living frugally and writing his *Treatise*. He published its first two parts in 1739, two years after his return, and the third part in 1740. Two volumes of essays, published in 1741 and 1742, did a little better. He applied unsuccessfully for a philosophical chair at Edinburgh and, in need of an income, became tutor for a year to the insane marquess of Annandale. In 1746 he accompanied General St Clair on an invasion of Brittany that was called off, and a little later went with St Clair to Vienna and Turin. His *Enquiry concerning Human Understanding*, a somewhat mutilating revision of book I of the *Treatise*, came out at this time, in 1749, and he returned to Scotland to finish its companion-piece, *Enquiry concerning the Principles of Morals*, his own favourite amongst his works.

From 1751 to 1757 Hume served as Keeper of the Advocates' Library in Edinburgh, the best library in the country, and ideally convenient for the major historical project that he now began, his six-volume *History of England*. The volumes on the Stuarts came out, to some controversy for trying to do justice to that family, in 1754 and 1756; those on the Tudors in 1759; those on the dynasties back to Julius Caesar in 1772. He visited London in 1758 and 1761, but his most satisfying foreign trip was his stay in Paris between 1763 and 1766 as secretary to the earl of Hertford. He was agreeably lionized by the *philosophes*, had a serious romance, of unknown intimacy, with the comtesse de Boufflers and saw a good deal of Rousseau, whom he brought back to refuge in England. Rousseau soon fled, spreading implausible paranoid fantasies about Hume.

His public career reached its high point with his appointment as under-secretary of state for the northern department between 1767 and 1769. This was the time of the last political gasp of the ageing, unhealthy and somewhat deranged William Pitt the elder. Hume seems to have given satisfaction. In 1769 he returned to Edinburgh and his circle of friends for eight happy final years. Before he died, of stomach cancer, in 1776 he had the pleasure of upsetting Boswell by his cheerful freedom from any fear of death.

Hume was a large man, gangling and bony in youth, but ever more corpulent and red in the face as the years went by. He was genial and kindly, good tempered and good company, an excellent friend and a placable enemy. He could see merit in an honest and serious opponent like Thomas Reid and mildly disposed of a fatuous one like James Beattie with the comment 'a silly, bigoted fellow'.

I was born the 26th of April, old style, at Edinburgh. I was of a good family, both by father and mother: my father's family is a branch of the Earl of Home's, or Hume's; and my ancestors had been proprietors of the estate, which my brother possesses, for several generations ... I passed through the ordinary course of education with success, and was seized very early with a passion for literature, which has been the ruling passion of my life, and the great source of my enjoyments. My studious disposition, my sobriety, and my industry, gave my family the notion that the law was a proper profession for me; but I found an unsurmountable aversion to everything but the pursuits of philosophy and general learning; and while they fancied I was poring upon Voet and Vinnius, Cicero and Virgil were the authors which I was secretly devouring. (Ess 607–8)

Never literary attempt was more unfortunate than my *Treatise of Human Nature*. It fell *dead-born from the press*, without reaching such distinction, as even to excite a murmur among the zealots. But being naturally of a cheerful and sanguine temper, I very soon recovered the blow, and prosecuted with great ardour my studies in the country. In 1742 I printed at Edinburgh the first part of my *Essays*: the work was favourably received, and soon made me entirely forget my former disappointment. I continued with my mother and brother in the country, and in that time recovered the knowledge of the Greek language which I had too much neglected in my early youth. (Ess 608–9)

But notwithstanding this variety of winds and seasons, to which my writings had been exposed, they had still been making such advances, that the copy-money given me by the booksellers, much exceeded any thing formerly known in England; I was become not only independent, but opulent. (Ess 613)

Those who have not seen the strange effects of modes, will never imagine the reception I met with at Paris, from men and women of all ranks and stations. The more I resiled from their excessive civilities, the more I was loaded with them. There is, however, a real satisfaction in living at Paris, from the great number of sensible, knowing and polite company with which that city abounds above all places in the universe. I thought once of settling there for life. (Ess 614)

To conclude historically with my own character. I am, or rather was (for that is the style I must now use in speaking of myself, which emboldens me the more to speak my sentiments); I was, I say, a man of mild dispositions, of command of temper, of an open, social and cheerful humour, capable of attachment, but little susceptible of enmity, and of great moderation in all my passions. Even my love of literary fame, my ruling passion, never soured my temper, notwithstanding my frequent disappointments. My company was not unacceptable to the young and careless, as well as to the studious and literary; and as I took a particular pleasure in the company of modest women, I had no reason to be displeased with the reception I met with from them. In a word, though most men anywise eminent, have found reason to complain of calumny, I never was touched, or even attacked by her baleful tooth; and though I wantonly exposed myself to the rage of both civil and religious factions, they seemed to be disarmed in my behalf of their wonted fury. My friends never had occasion to vindicate any one circumstance of my character and conduct; not but that the zealots, we may well suppose, would have been glad to invent and propagate any story to my disadvantage, but they could never find any which they thought would wear the face of probability. I cannot say there is no vanity in making this funeral oration of myself, but I hope it is not a misplaced one; and this is a matter of fact which is easily cleared and ascertained. (Ess 615–16)

PHILOSOPHICAL ASSUMPTIONS

Hume is doubly an empiricist. First, he regards philosophy as an empirical science. That position is announced in the subtitle of the *Treatise*: 'an attempt to introduce the experimental method of reasoning into moral subjects'. The experimental method is what Newton's sublime achievement is based on (but mathematics had a lot to do with it too), so Hume is reasonably credited with the ambition of being the Newton of the moral (i.e. human) sciences. To a considerable extent his procedure is in accord with this declaration of intent. He seeks to show how the complex detail of our intellectual life arises in accordance with the laws of association from its primary elements, the atoms of thought he calls impressions and ideas. But it is not for this general cognitive psychology on associationist principles that he is usually regarded as important.

Secondly, he is an empiricist in a more familiar sense. He maintains that all the raw material of our thoughts and beliefs comes from experience, sensory and introspective. He in fact applies this principle as a criterion of significance. Our thoughts are without content, and our words without meaning, unless they are connected to experience. He also holds that most of our knowledge rests on experience or, since the only certain knowledge we have is mathematical and concerned with the relations of ideas, that what we acceptably believe does. It might seem he was committed to his view that philosophy is an empirical science by his view that all factual belief is empirical. But that does not follow. Most modern sympathizers with Hume would say that philosophy, 'true' philosophy, is conceptual, not factual, as much a business of examining the relations of ideas as mathematics is.

He boldly asserts that philosophy is the first or master science. All sciences or bodies of professed knowledge are the work of the human understanding. Therefore the study of the human understanding is prior to all the others. Where Newton, in Hume's view, had explained the material universe by means of the law of gravitational attraction, his aim is to explain the workings of the mind by a parallel law of association.

The raw materials of thought, which is the work of the understanding, are impressions and their varyingly lively copies, ideas. Impressions are either of sensation, such as colours and sounds, or reflection, such as emotions and desires. They may also be simple – homogeneous and unanalysable – or complex. Every simple idea presupposes a corresponding simple impression. Complex ideas need not do so: we would all recognize a dragon if we came across one.

Ideas are distinguished from impressions by their lesser vivacity. If they are not at all lively, they are ideas of the imagination. If they are more lively, and retain their 'form and order', they are ideas of memory. Of the same degree of liveliness, it appears, are ideas of expectation, which are the elementary form of our causal beliefs. Belief is a feature of ideas of memory and expectation, as contrasted with mere imaginings. It is not a further idea, since, if so, it could be added to any other idea, however fantastic, and produce a belief in it. A related point, made at a later stage, is that there is no idea of existence. The idea of a thing is the same as the idea of that thing as existing. Presumably Hume would establish the empirical credentials of existence by saying that it is present in every impression, since impressions involve the infallible awareness of something (even if only a coloured patch in one's private field of vision).

Hume admits that his principle of the universal dependence of impressions on ideas is imperfect. One might recognize a shade of blue one had never met with, only its close neighbours on the spectrum. That is an unnecessary admission. The missing shade could be seen as a complex idea made of the blue next door to it and the idea, well exemplified empirically, of 'a little more blue than'.

There is much that is more seriously wrong with Hume's account of impressions and ideas than that. For him an idea is a mental picture or image. We do think in images to some extent, but we also think in words, and in diagrams and schemas, which are in a way image-like, although hardly copies. The crucial point is that all these items are the vehicles of concepts or meanings. It is easy to think of imaginings (hallucinations and dreams, for example) that are much more lively than most of what we perceive, let alone remember.

Hume's view that images are the primary vehicles of thought may have been assisted by his commitment to Berkeley's rejection of 'abstract ideas'. An impression is of one, particular, wholly determinate thing. How do we think of it as one of a kind, as having some general term truly applied to it? Locke thought we abstract the qualities common to all oranges and use the resulting abstract idea to recognize a particular orange as an orange. Berkeley rejected this, since different oranges have incompatible qualities. We use a particular image to 'represent' all the members of the kind. But in any one image a host of kinds will be representable: oranges, but also round things, orange-coloured things and so on. Hume coped with this by saying that when we allocate something to a kind because of its similarity to some standard image, we have a lot of other images at our disposal which we can bring to mind to guide our classification along the right path.

Finally, in this first part of the *Treatise*, Hume anticipates points he will develop more fully later in discussing material objects and persons, by a general dismissal of the legitimacy of the idea of substance. There is no impression from which it can be derived. All we perceive is collections of qualities, persistently associated with each other. If substance is defined as that which is capable of independent existence, then the only substances are impressions and ideas.

It is evident, that all the sciences have a relation, greater or less, to human nature; and that, however wide any of them may seem to run from it, they still return back by one passage or another. Even *Mathematics, Natural*

Philosophy and *Natural Religion* are in some measure dependent on the science of MAN; since they lie under the cognisance of men, and are judged of by their powers and faculties ... If, the sciences of Mathematics, Natural Philosophy, and Natural Religion, have such a dependence on the knowledge of man, what may be expected in the other sciences, whose connection with human nature is more close and intimate? (T xix)

There is no question of importance, whose decision is not comprised in the science of man; and there is none, which can be decided with any certainty, before we become acquainted with that science. In pretending, therefore, to explain the principles of human nature, we in effect propose a complete system of the sciences, built on a foundation, and the only one upon which they can stand with any security. And as the science of man is the only solid foundation for the other sciences, so the only solid foundation we can give to this science itself must be laid on experience and observation. (T xix-xx)

All the perceptions of the human mind resolve themselves into two distinct kinds, which I shall call *impressions* and *ideas*. The difference betwixt these consists in the degrees of force and liveliness, with which they strike upon the mind, and make their way into our thought and consciousness. Those perceptions which enter with most force and violence, we may name *impressions*; and under this name I comprehend all our sensations, passions and emotions, as they make their first appearance in the soul. By *ideas* I mean the faint images of these in thinking and reasoning; such as, for instance, are all the perceptions excited by the present discourse, excepting only those which arise from the sight and touch, and excepting the immediate pleasure or uneasiness it may occasion. I believe it will not be necessary to employ many words in explaining this distinction. Every one of himself will readily perceive the difference betwixt feeling and thinking. (T 1)

Every simple idea has a simple impression which resembles it, and every simple impression a correspondent idea. (T 3)

A very material question has been started concerning *abstract* or *general* ideas, *whether they be general or particular in the mind's conception of them*. A great Philosopher [Berkeley] has disputed the received opinion in this particular and has asserted, that all general ideas are nothing but particular ones annexed to a certain term, which gives them a more extensive signification, and makes them recall upon occasion other individuals, which are similar to them. As I look upon this to be one of the greatest and most valuable discoveries that has been made in late years in the republic of letters, I shall here endeavour to confirm it by some arguments, which I hope will put it beyond all doubt and controversy.

It is evident, that in forming most of our general ideas, if not all of them, we abstract from every particular degree of quality and quantity, and that an object ceases not to be of any particular species on account of every small alteration in its extension, duration and other properties. It may, therefore, be thought, that here is a plain dilemma, that decides concerning the nature of those abstract ideas, which have afforded so much speculation to philosophers. The abstract idea of a man represents men of all sizes and all qualities, which it is concluded it cannot do, but either by representing at once all possible sizes and all possible qualities, or by representing no particular one at all. Now it having been esteemed absurd to defend the former proposition, as implying an infinite capacity in the mind, it has been commonly inferred in favour of the latter; and our abstract ideas have been supposed to represent no particular degree either of quantity or quality. But that this inference is erroneous, I shall endeavour to make appear, *first*, by proving, that it is utterly impossible to conceive any quantity or quality, without forming a precise notion of its degrees; and, *secondly*, by showing, that though the capacity of the mind be not infinite, yet we can at once form a notion of all possible quantity and quality, in such a manner at least, as, however imperfect, may serve all the purposes of reflection and conversation. (T 17–18)

All the objects of human reason or enquiry may naturally be divided into two kinds, to wit, *Relations of Ideas* and *Matters of Fact*. Of the first kind are the sciences of Geometry, Algebra and Arithmetic; in short every affirmation which is either intuitively or demonstratively certain. *That the square of the hypotenuse is equal to the square of the two sides*, is a proposition which expresses the relation between these figures, *That three times five is equal to the half of thirty*, expresses a relation between these numbers. Propositions of this kind are discoverable by the mere operation of thought, without dependence on what is anywhere existent in the universe. Though there never were a circle or triangle in nature, the truths demonstrated by Euclid would for ever retain their certainty and evidence.

Matters of fact, which are the second objects of human reason, are not ascertained in the same manner; nor is our evidence of their truth, however great, of a like nature with the foregoing. The contrary of every matter of fact is still possible; because it can never imply a contradiction, and is conceived by the mind, with the same facility and distinctness, as if ever so conformable to reality. *That the sun will not rise tomorrow* is no less intelligible a proposition and implies no more contradiction than the affirmation *that it will rise*. (E 25–6)

CAUSATION

Hume's account of causation is, rightly, the best-known and the most influential part of his philosophy. Where others of his leading contentions are at best interestingly provocative, it remains a compelling object of concern for philosophers. He treats it as a relation between objects before he sets out his disconcertingly sceptical views about our knowledge of objects, but that is because he takes all our beliefs about matters of fact, in so far as they go beyond the impressions that are immediately present to the mind, as all but the most elementary do, to be the outcome of causal inference. That is not strictly correct. The sweet taste that I infer to be obtainable from the orange I see is neither the cause nor the effect of the seen orange. But it is still a 'distinct existence', which could have failed to occur even though the orange was present. Factual inference, of which causal inference is a primary example, is the universal link between the observed and the unobserved, between what we perceive to happen and what must have happened or must be going to happen.

Being a cause, or an effect, is not a quality of things, like being red or round. If it were, it would be a property of everything, like existence, and we should have no impression of it. It is, plainly enough, a relation: a complex, threefold one, composed of contiguity in space and time, succession and necessary connection. Neither contiguity nor succession is, in fact, essential to causation. There can be action at a distance and cause and effect can be simultaneous (Hume has an ingenious but invalid argument to prove that they cannot be). The matter is not important and most straightforward examples of causal relationship do have contiguous and successive terms, anyway. It is not important, since contiguity and succession are empirically unproblematic; we have impressions of both. Necessary connection is the indispensable but irksome ingredient. However closely we examine an alleged

16

instance of causal relationship (the cue ball coming into contact with the red and the red shooting off to the pocket), we observe no necessary connection between them, although we believe there is one.

Hume poses two questions. Why do we think that every event must have a cause and why do we think that each particular cause must have the effect we take it to have? The general causal principle is neither self-evident nor provable. He disposes with typical neatness of some attempted proofs. Locke, for example, said that if the principle were false, something would have been caused by nothing; but nothing is far too weak to have caused anything. This anticipation of Lewis Carroll is easily shown to beg the question. Nor can it be proved that any particular event is the cause of what is taken to be its effect. Cause and effect are distinct existences; it is therefore never a contradiction to suppose that one occurred and the other did not.

Where we believe two kinds of event to be causally related, we believe them to be constantly conjoined at all times on the basis of our remembering them to have been constantly conjoined in our experience. The inference from the limited conjunction that we have observed to the universal conjunction that our causal belief embodies assumes that the unobserved resembles the observed or, more vaguely, that nature is uniform. But this, like the general principle, is neither self-evident nor provable. The unobserved is 'distinct' from the observed; its taking any form whatever is compatible with the observed being the way it is. Nor can it be established inductively on the evidence that hitherto, at any rate, the unobserved has largely resembled the observed. To do that would be to argue in a circle, to assume its validity in its own proof.

Tucked away in a discussion of probability is an interesting distinction between probable conclusions based on insufficient evidence (I have met five Dutchmen and they all like eels) and that based on contrary evidence (I have met a hundred Dutchmen and ninety-five of them like eels). In either case, coming across a new Dutchman, I shall conclude that he probably likes eels, but shall claim no more than that. In the second case I am relying on the general proposition that nineteen out of twenty Dutchmen like eels, which is the product of an inductive inference from the proportion of eel-fanciers I have observed. Hume's criticism, then, is not to be circumvented by arguing that nature is probably uniform or that the unobserved will probably resemble the observed, if it is the second kind of probability that is in question. For that can only be based on the constancy of observed frequencies or proportions. But the first kind of probability, which Hume brushes aside as figuring only in early life, which is surely incorrect, is not open to that objection. It has been argued that 'if all known As are Bs then it is probable that (i.e. there is some, if insufficient, evidence that) all As whatever are Bs' is demonstrable. It is because of the *meaning* of the word 'evidence' that the quoted statement about As and Bs is true; it states an 'abstract relation of ideas' not a matter of fact.

Hume, at any rate, convinced that the inductive inference which is embodied in our causal beliefs, and all other factual beliefs that go beyond present impressions, cannot be rationally justified, turns to explaining how it is that we inveterately have recourse to it. His answer is that our experience of constant conjunction, through the influence of association, leads us, as a matter of custom or habit, to have a lively expectation of a window's shattering when we observe a brick flying towards it. The impression from which our idea of necessary connection is derived is not of sensation, but of reflection, that of feeling compelled in expecting the broken window on perception of the brick flying towards it.

He concludes his main account of the subject by putting forward two definitions of 'cause' which are of two quite different, if not unrelated, things. The first is in terms of the constant conjunction of the two factors, the second is in terms of the impression of one factor determining the mind to form a lively idea of the other. The second of these seems to state what Hume thinks goes on in our minds when we form or have a causal belief; the first of them to state what we actually believe. They cannot both be correct. The first is what we believe; the second explains the belief and, perhaps, states all we are entitled to believe.

Until the twentieth century most commentators on Hume took him to be, whether seriously or frivolously, a complete sceptic about causal and inductive beliefs (and a good many other things). But he does set out 'rules for judging causes and effects', clearly takes it to be true that every event has a cause (for example, in insisting that chance events are really all the effects of unknown causes) and, of course, himself indulges in a great deal of inductive inference in his application of the 'experimental method' to the workings of the human mind.

> All reasonings concerning matter of fact seem to be founded on the relation of *Cause and Effect*. By means of that relation alone we can go beyond the evidence of our memory and senses. If you were to ask a man, why he believes any matter of fact, which is absent; for instance, that his friend is in the country, or in France; he would give you a reason; and this reason would be some other fact; as a letter received from him, or the knowledge of his former resolutions and promises. A man finding a watch or any other machine in a desert island, would conclude that there had once been men in that island. All our reasonings concerning fact are of the same nature. And here it is constantly supposed that there is a connexion between the present fact and that which is inferred from it. Were there nothing to bind them together, the inference would be entirely precarious. (E 26–7)

> If we would satisfy ourselves, therefore, concerning the nature of that evidence, which assures us of matters of fact, we must enquire how we arrive at the knowledge of cause and effect.
>
> I shall venture to affirm, as a general proposition, which admits of no exception, that the knowledge of this relation is not, in any instance, attained by reasonings *a priori*; but arises entirely from experience, when we find that any particular objects are constantly

conjoined with each other. Let an object be presented to a man of ever so strong natural reason and abilities; if that object be entirely new to him, he will not to able, by the most accurate examination of its sensible qualities, to discover any of its causes or effects. Adam, though his rational faculties be supposed, at the very first, entirely perfect, could not have inferred from the fluency and transparency of water that it would suffocate him, or from the light and warmth of fire that it would consume him. No object ever discovers, by the qualities which appear to the senses, either the causes which produced it, or the effects which will arise from it; nor can our reason, unassisted by experience, ever draw any inference concerning real existence and matter of fact. (E 27)

Let us therefore cast our eye on any two objects, which we call cause and effect, and turn them on all sides, in order to find that impression, which produces an idea of such prodigious consequence. At first sight I perceive, that I must not search for it in any of the particular *qualities* of the objects; since, whichever of these qualities I pitch on, I find some object that is not possessed of it, and yet falls under the denomination of cause or effect. And indeed there is nothing existent, either externally or internally, which is not to be considered either as a cause or an effect; though it is plain that there is no one quality which universally belongs to all beings, and gives them a title to that denomination.

The idea then of causation must be derived from some *relation* among objects; and that relation we must now endeavour to discover. I find in the first place, that whatever objects are considered as causes or effects, are *contiguous*; and that nothing can operate in a time or place, which is ever so little removed from those of its existence. Though distant objects may sometimes seem productive of each other, that are commonly found upon examination to be linked by a chain of causes, which are contiguous among themselves, and to the distant objects; and when in any particular instance we cannot discover this connection, we still presume it to exist. We may therefore consider the relation of *contiguity* as essential to that of causation; at least may suppose it such, according to the general opinion, till we can find a more proper occasion to clear up this matter, by examining what objects are or are not susceptible of juxtaposition and conjunction.

The second relation I shall observe as essential to causes and effects, is not so universally acknowledged, but is liable to some controversy. It is that of *priority* of time in the cause before the effect. Some pretend that it is not absolutely necessary a cause should precede its effect; but that any object or action, in the very first moment of its existence, may exert its productive quality, and give rise to another object or action, perfectly contemporary with itself. But beside that experience in most instances seems to contradict this opinion, we may establish the relation of priority by a kind of inference or reasoning. It is an established maxim, both in natural and moral philosophy, that an object, which exists for any time in its full perfection without producing another, is not its sole cause; but is assisted by some other principle which pushes it from its state of inactivity, and makes it exert that energy, of which it was secretly possessed. Now if any cause be perfectly contemporary with its effect, it is certain, according to this maxim, that they must all of them be so; since any one of them, which retards its operation for a single moment, exerts not itself at that very individual time, in which it might have operated; and therefore is no proper cause. The consequence of this would be no less than the destruction of that succession of causes, which we observe in the world; and indeed the utter annihilation of time. For if one cause were contemporary with its effect, and this effect with *its* effect and so on, it is plain there would be no such thing as succession, and all objects must be co-existent.

If this argument appear satisfactory, it is well. If not, I beg the reader to allow me the same liberty, which I have used in the preceding case, of supposing it such. For he shall find, that the affair is of no great importance.

Having thus discovered or supposed the two relations of *contiguity* and *succession* to be essential to causes and effects, I find I am stopped short, and can proceed no further in considering any single instance of cause and effect. Motion in one body is regarded upon impulse as cause of motion in another. When we consider these objects with the utmost attention, we find only that the one body approaches the other; and the motion of it precedes that of the other, but without any sensible interval. It is in vain to rack ourselves with *further* thought and reflection upon this subject. We can go no further in considering this particular instance.

We must therefore proceed like those who, being in search of anything that lies concealed from them, and not finding it in the place they expected, beat about all the neighbouring fields, without any certain view or design, in hopes their good fortune will at last guide them to what they search for. It is necessary for us to leave the direct survey of this question concerning the nature of that *necessary connection*, which enters into our idea of cause and effect; and endeavour to find some other questions, the examination of which will perhaps afford a hint, that may serve to clear up the present difficulty. Of these questions there occur two, which I shall proceed to examine, viz.

First, for what reason we pronounce it *necessary*, that everything whose existence has a beginning, should also have a cause?

Secondly, why we conclude, that such particular causes must *necessarily* have such particular effects; and what is the nature of that *inference* we draw from the one to the other, and of the belief we repose in it? (T 77–8)

We can never demonstrate the necessity of a cause to every new existence, or new modification of existence, without showing at the same time the impossibility there is, that anything can ever begin to exist without some productive principle; and where the latter proposition cannot be proved, we must despair of ever being able to prove the former. Now that the latter proposition is utterly incapable of a demonstrative proof, we may satisfy ourselves by considering, that as all distinct ideas are separable from each other, and as the ideas of cause and effect are evidently distinct, it will be easy for us to conceive any object to be non-existent this moment, and existent the next, without conjoining to it the distinct idea of a cause or productive principle. The separation therefore of the idea of a cause from that of a beginning of existence, is plainly possible for the imagination; and consequently the actual separation of these objects is so far possible, that it implies no contradiction nor absurdity; and is therefore incapable of being refuted by any reasoning from mere ideas, without which it is impossible to demonstrate the necessity of a cause. (T 79–80)

It is therefore by experience only that we can infer the existence of one object from that of another. The nature of experience is this. We remember to have had frequent instances of the existence of one species of objects, and also remember, that the individuals of another species of objects have always attended them, and have existed in a regular order of contiguity and succession with regard to them. Thus we remember to have seen that species of object we call *flame*, and to have felt that species of sensation we call *heat*. We likewise call to mind their constant conjunction in all past instances. Without any further ceremony, we call the one *cause*, and the other *effect*, and infer the existence of the one from that of the other. In all those instances from which we learn the conjunction of particular causes and effects, both the causes and effects have been perceived by the senses, and are remembered, but in all cases, wherein we reason concerning them, there is only one perceived or remembered, and the other is supplied in conformity to our past experience.

Thus in advancing we have insensibly discovered a new relation betwixt cause and effect when we least expected it, and were entirely employed upon another subject. This relation is their *constant conjunction*. Contiguity and succession are not sufficient to make us pronounce any two objects to be cause and effect, unless we perceive that these two relations are preserved in several instances. We may now see the advantage of quitting the direct survey of this relation, in order to discover the nature of that *necessary connection* which makes so essential a part of it. (T 86–7)

Having thus explained the manner *in which we reason beyond our immediate impressions, and conclude that such particular causes must have such particular effects*; we must now return upon our footsteps to examine that question which first occurred to us, and which we dropped in our way, viz. *What is our idea of necessity, when we say that two objects are necessarily connected together?* Upon this head I repeat, what I have often had occasion to observe, that as we have no idea that is not derived from an impression, we must find some impression that gives rise to this idea of necessity. (T 155)

[We must] repeat to ourselves that the simple view of any two objects or actions, however related, can never give us any idea of power, or of a connection betwixt them; *that* this idea arises from the repetition of their union; *that* the repetition neither discovers nor causes anything in the objects, but has an influence only on the mind, by that customary transition it produces; *that* this customary transition is therefore the same with the power and necessity; which are consequently qualities of perceptions, not of objects, and are internally felt by the soul, and not perceived externally in bodies. (T 166)

We may define a *cause* to be 'An object precedent and contiguous to another, and where all the objects resembling the former are placed in like relations of precedency and contiguity to those objects that resemble the latter'. If this definition be esteemed defective, because drawn from objects foreign to the cause, we may substitute this other definition in its place, viz. 'A cause is an object precedent and contiguous to another, and so united with it, that the idea of the one determines the mind to form the idea, and the impression of the one to form a more lively idea of the other'. (T 170)

MATERIAL THINGS

Having argued that all beliefs in matters of fact – apart from our immediate awareness of our current impressions and, presumably, memories of them – rests on causal belief, Hume has tried to show that such beliefs are not justified. They are justified neither by experience, since we have no impression of necessary connection, nor by reason, since the contradictory either of any general causal or inductive principle or of any particular causal belief is possible. All we can hope to do is to explain how we come to have the causal beliefs we do, and make the predictions to which they lead us, namely by experience of constant conjunction which instils in us a habit of expectation.

Much the same strategy is employed in his accounts of our belief in an external world of material things and our belief in ourselves as continuing existences. He opens his discussion of material things by distinguishing two questions. One of these, the question *'whether there be body or not?'*, is, he says, 'vain to ask'. However, 'we may well ask *What causes induce us to believe in the existence of body?'* To believe in the existence of body, or material things, is to believe in something that has continued and distinct existence, something that exists at times when we have no impressions of it and which, therefore, exists independently of us. It is a plain contradiction to suppose that the senses reveal to us the existence of unperceived things (or unperceived tracts of their history). Nor can the belief be based on causal inference from our impressions, which is what it amounts to in these circumstances, as in the 'modern philosophy' of Locke. We cannot experience a constant conjunction between the perceived and the unperceived, let alone compare one with another to discover the (partial) resemblance that Locke asserts to obtain between them.

The question 'whether there be body or not' turns out to be 'vain' in two ways. Since neither experience nor reason can answer it, we can give no justified answer to the question. But he also says that 'nature has not left this to [our] choice and has doubtless esteemed it an affair of too great importance to be trusted to our uncertain reasonings and speculations'. We cannot justify our belief in a world of continued and distinct material things, but we cannot help holding such a belief. What we can do is explain how it is forced upon us. The explanation lies in the constancy and coherence displayed by the impressions of the senses. We leave the dining-table to look out of the window and when we come back things just like the things that appeared on the dining-table appear there once more (constancy). The fire that was blazing in the hearth when we went out to make a long telephone call is now just smouldering in the way that continuously observed fires have been seen to die down steadily on other occasions (coherence).

The ordinary, 'vulgar', view of the matter 'feigns' or imagines unperceived perceptions to fill the steady or graduated gaps. That is a contradiction, but the unreflective mind passes over that. The 'system of the philosophers' (i.e. Locke) is even worse, since it supposes the existence of things that are neither causally related to nor like the impressions held to testify to their existence.

We may well ask, *What causes induce us to believe in the existence of body?* but it is in vain to ask, *Whether there be body or not?* That is a point we must take for granted in all our reasonings.

The subject, then, of our present inquiry, is concerning the *causes* which induce us to believe in the existence of body; and my reasonings on this head I shall begin with a distinction, which at first sight may seem superfluous, but which will contribute very much to the perfect understanding of what follows. We ought to examine apart those two questions, which are commonly confounded together, viz. Why we attribute a *continued* existence to objects, even when they are not present to the senses; and why we suppose them to have an existence distinct from the mind and perception? Under this last head I comprehend their situation as well as relations, their *external* position as well as the independence of their existence and operation. (T 186–7)

That our senses offer not their impressions as the images of something *distinct*, or *independent*, and *external*, is evident; because they convey to us nothing but a single perception, and never give us the least intimation of anything beyond. A single perception can never produce the idea of a double existence, but by some influence of the reason or imagination. When the mind looks further than what immediately appears to it, its conclusions can never be put to the account of the senses; and it certainly looks further, when from a single perception it infers a double existence, and supposes the relations of resemblance and causation betwixt them. (T 189)

We may observe, then, that it is neither upon account of the involuntariness of certain impressions, as is commonly supposed, nor of their superior force and violence, that we attribute to them a reality and continued existence, which we refuse to others, that are voluntary or feeble. For it is evident our pains and pleasures, our passions and affections, which we never suppose to have any existence beyond our perception, are equally involuntary, as the impressions of figure and extension, colour and sound which we suppose to be permanent beings. The heat of a fire, when moderate, is supposed to exist in the fire; but the pain which it causes on a near approach is not taken to have any being except in the perception.

These vulgar opinions, then, being rejected, we must search for some other hypothesis, by which we may discover those peculiar qualities in our impressions, which make us attribute to them a distinct and continued existence.

After a little examination, we shall find that all those objects, to which we attribute a continued existence, have a peculiar *constancy*, which distinguishes them from the impressions whose existence depends upon our perception. Those mountains, and houses, and trees, which lie at present under my eye, have always appeared to me in the same order; and when I lose sight of them by shutting my eyes or turning my head, I soon after find them return upon me without the least alteration. My bed and table, my books and papers, present themselves in the same uniform manner, and change not upon account of an interruption in my seeing or perceiving them. This is the case with all the impressions whose objects are supposed to have an external existence; and is the case with no other impressions, whether gentle or violent, voluntary or involuntary.

This constancy, however, is not so perfect as not to admit of very considerable exceptions. Bodies often change their position and qualities, and, after a little absence or interruption, may become hardly knowable. But here it is observable, that even in these changes they preserve a *coherence*, and have a regular dependence on each other; which is the foundation of a kind of reasoning from causation, and produces the opinion of their continued existence. When I return to my chamber after an hour's absence, I find not my fire in the same situation in which I left it; but then I am accustomed, in other instances, to see a like alteration produced in a like time, whether I am present or absent, near or remote. This coherence, therefore, in their changes, is one of the characteristics of external objects, as well as their constancy. (T 194–5)

THE SELF

The self, conceived as something with a continuous identity through time, also falls victim to Hume's characteristic two-pronged style of attack. I know that I am now having certain experiences and I remember having had others. But I have no impression of an unchanging item to which all these things belong. Since it would have to be an unalterable, invariant content of my consciousness, it could not make itself felt. It would have the empirically elusive character of existence. In fact, Hume argues, whenever I look most closely into myself all I can find is a more or less chaotic sequence of particular perceptions, impressions and ideas of sensation and reflection, feelings and thoughts.

On the other hand, reason no more requires than experience does the supposition of a persisting bearer of my identity through time, a support for my varying experiences to inhere in. Each experience or 'perception' is a distinct existence from whose existence that of no other thing necessarily follows. That is, of all Hume's bold eliminations, the one that other philosophers have found it hardest to swallow. Does he not refute himself when he says 'for my part, when I enter most intimately into what I call *myself*, I always stumble on some particular perception or other'? What is this I that is doing the entering? J.S. Mill and others have thought it impossible that a mere series could be aware of itself as a series. Against that it could be argued that a present state of consciousness could contain or be a recollection of previous states of consciousness somehow related to it.

Indeed it has seemed to many, particularly Locke, that memory, in the sense of direct personal recollection, is the relation that connects a temporally spread-out bundle of experiences or mental states into a single, continuous self, mind or person. Hume rejected this theory, relying on

Butler's argument that, as Hume puts it, memory does not constitute, but discovers, personal identity. I cannot judge that some idea is one of memory, rather than imagination, unless I have first found out that the experience supposedly remembered was an experience of *mine*.

Hume remained unsatisfied with the account of the relation which unites a series of experiences into a self that he gave in the *Treatise*, which was that it is a compound of resemblance and causation. Perhaps Butler's argument is a bit too swift. To decide that some past experience is one's own and that the idea one has of it is an idea of memory are not two things, of which the first has to precede the second; they seem much more like one and the same thing.

He has a long and entangled argument about the immateriality of the soul, a theologian's thesis which he mischievously assimilates to the monism of Spinoza. It turns on the view that the soul is an immaterial substance. But one can take the soul or self, even if conceived not as a substance but as a series, to be non-material, as Hume appears to do, and that leaves open the possibility of its survival of the death of the body. He takes up the problem in an attractive essay. If our minds are made of some spiritual stuff, why should that stuff not make up different minds in the way that matter enters into the composition of different bodies? Furthermore, 'the soul, if immortal, existed before our birth; and if the former existence noways concerned us, neither will the latter'.

There are some philosophers who imagine we are every moment intimately conscious of what we call our *self*; that we feel its existence and its continuance in existence; and are certain, beyond the evidence of a demonstration, both of its perfect identity and simplicity. The strongest sensation, the most violent passion, say they, instead of distracting us from this view, only fix it the more intensely and make us consider their influence on *self* either by their pain or pleasure. To attempt a further proof of this were to weaken its evidence; since no proof can be derived from any fact of which we are so intimately conscious; nor is there anything of which we can be certain if we doubt of this.

Unluckily all these positive assertions are contrary to that very experience which is pleaded for them; nor have we any idea of *self*, after the manner it is here explained. For from what impression could this idea be derived? This question is impossible to answer without a manifest contradiction and absurdity; and yet it is a question which must necessarily be answered, if we would have the idea of self pass for clear and intelligible. It must be some one impression that gives rise to every real idea. But self or person is not any one impression, but that to which our several impressions and ideas are supposed to have a reference. If any impression gives rise to the idea of self, that impression must continue invariably the same, through the whole course of our lives; since self is supposed to exist after that manner. But there is no impression constant and invariable. Pain and pleasure, grief and joy, passions and sensations succeed each other, and never all exist at the same time. It cannot therefore be from any of these impressions, or from any other, that the idea of self is derived; and consequently there is no such idea. (T 251–2)

I may venture to affirm of the rest of mankind that they are nothing but a bundle or collection of different perceptions, which succeed each other with an inconceivable rapidity, and are in a perpetual flux and movement. Our eyes cannot turn in their sockets without varying our perceptions. Our thought is still more variable than our sight; and all our other senses and faculties contribute to this change; nor is there any single power of the soul, which remains unalterably the same, perhaps for one moment. The mind is a kind of theatre, where several perceptions successively make their appearance; pass, repass, glide away, and mingle in an infinite variety of postures and situations. There is properly no *simplicity* in it at one time, nor *identity* in different, whatever natural propension we may have to imagine that simplicity and identity. The comparison of the theatre must not mislead us. They are the successive perceptions only, that constitute the mind; nor have we the most distant notion of the place where these scenes are represented, or of the materials of which it is composed. (T 252–3)

As memory alone acquaints us with the continuance and extent of this succession of perceptions, it is to be considered, upon that account chiefly, as the source of personal identity. Had we no memory, we never should have any notion of causation, nor consequently of that chain of causes and effects, which constitute our self or person. But having once acquired this notion of causation from the memory, we can extend the same chain of causes, and consequently the identity of our persons beyond our memory, and can comprehend times, and circumstances, and actions, which we have entirely forgot, but suppose in general to have existed. For how few of our past actions are there, of which we have any memory? Who can tell me, for instance, what were his thoughts and actions on the first of January 1715, the eleventh of March 1719, and the third of August 1733? Or will he affirm, because he has entirely forgot the incidents of these days, that the present self is not the same person with the self of that time; and by that means overturn all the most established notions of personal identity? In this view, therefore, memory does not so much *produce* as *discover* personal identity, by showing us the relation of cause and effect among our different perceptions. It will be incumbent on those who affirm that memory produces entirely our personal identity, to give a reason why we can thus extend our identity beyond our memory. (T 261–2)

SCEPTICISM

The traditional view of Hume, as was mentioned earlier, takes him to be an extreme sceptic, to have undermined the claims to validity of the whole body of our beliefs in the external world, the self and causation. More recently, the idea has gained ground that he has sceptically established the limits of rational justification, turned reason on itself, in order to show that these beliefs are nevertheless natural, instinctive and inevitable. In explaining how we in fact come to have the beliefs that we do, he shows that we are so constituted that we cannot help having them. After all, unless there were something to be said for them, what does he think he is doing in explaining them, since explanation is a matter of bringing things under causal laws?

Interpretation of Hume is made difficult by a kind of oscillation between two moods in which he contemplates the results of his own investigations. In one of them he looks on them with depression and despair, not knowing which way to turn. In the other, more cheerfully, he observes that as soon as we reimmerse ourselves in everyday life, the injuries inflicted by reason on itself fade away and we comfortably fall back into our customary, natural habits of belief. We should not seek to find some external support for these habits, which is a quest doomed to depressing failure. We should carry on with them in a chastened way, realizing that there is no certainty outside the realm of the abstract relations of ideas and marginally regulating them by adhering to the 'settled principles of the understanding' and avoiding wild, superstitious, ways of believing.

Analytic philosophers in the twentieth century (anticipated by J.S. Mill) took the features of our experience, which Hume used to explain our beliefs in objects, selves and causes, rather as defining what those beliefs, despite first appearances, actually amount to. They have defined objects as systems of actual and possible impressions, whose structure is intimated by the constant and coherent bits that are actually experienced (phenomenalism), selves as related series of mental events (the bundle theory) and causality as regular succession (the regularity theory). That is less disconcertingly sceptical than Hume's position. But this strategy leaves us with what seems to be a seriously diminished residue of what we originally believed. What is more, in the case of objects and causes, since belief in them, even in its attenuated form, is an open, generalized inference from partial evidence, it remains exposed to doubt about induction.

It has been suggested that Hume was really interested more in the concrete, practical topics of the later books of the *Treatise* than in the theoretical philosophy of book I, in morals, politics and psychology rather than in the theory of knowledge. As a pyrotechnical display of the limits of our minds as sources of certain knowledge, its purpose was to incapacitate dogmatism in those regions of belief where the passions were strongly involved.

> This sceptical doubt, both with respect to reason and the senses, is a malady which can never be radically cured, but must return upon us every moment, however we may chase it away, and sometimes seem entirely free from it. It is impossible, on any system, to defend either our understanding or senses; and we but expose them further when we endeavour to justify them in that manner. As the sceptical doubt arises naturally from a profound and intense reflection on those subjects, it always increases the further we carry our reflections, whether in opposition or conformity to it. Carelessness and inattention alone can afford us any remedy. For this reason I rely entirely upon them; and take it for granted, whatever may be the reader's opinion at this present moment, that an hour hence he will be persuaded there is both an external and internal world. (T 218)

The *intense* view of these manifold contradictions and imperfections in human reason has so wrought upon me, and heated my brain, that I am ready to reject all belief and reasoning, and can look upon no opinion even as more probable or likely than another. Where am I, or what? From what causes do I derive my existence, and to what condition shall I return? Whose favour shall I court, and whose anger must I dread? What beings surround me? and on whom have I any influence, or who have any influence on me? I am confounded with all these questions, and begin to fancy myself in the most deplorable condition imaginable, environed with the deepest darkness, and utterly deprived of the use of every member and faculty.

Most fortunately it happens, that since reason is incapable of dispelling these clouds, Nature herself suffices to that purpose, and cures me of this philosophical melancholy and delirium, either by relaxing this bent of mind, or by some avocation, and lively impression of my senses, which obliterate all these chimeras. I dine, I play a game of backgammon, I converse, and am merry with my friends; and when, after three or four hours' amusement, I would return to these speculations, they appear so cold, and strained, and ridiculous, that I cannot find in my heart to enter into them any further. (T 268–9)

MORALITY AND THE PASSIONS

Hume devoted the second of the three books of the *Treatise* to the passions. In this he was following the example of his great systematic predecessors, Descartes, Hobbes and Spinoza. But where their procedure was analytic, almost algebraic, a matter of classifying feelings and emotions and then going on to define the bulk of them in terms of such elemental items as pleasure, pain and desire, his was more descriptive and psychologically explanatory. Although full of bright ideas, his discussion is, on the whole, tedious and meandering, a riot of associationist speculation, relieved here and there, nevertheless, with flashes of insight. It has never provoked the interest and discussion excited by his accounts of knowledge and morality.

But there are three important things in his exposition. The first is a set of large, general distinctions within the field it covers. Passions are distinguished as violent or calm (which shows that he does not mean what we do by 'passion', namely violent emotion), as direct (that is, natural or instinctive) or indirect, and as strong or weak. A calm passion (such as prudence) can overcome and so show itself to be stronger than a violent one (such as lust). Secondly, there is an interesting and influential treatment of the problem of the freedom of the will. Thirdly, and most important for the theory of morality that is to follow, he insists that reason is 'inert', that it can never, on its own, and without the support of passion, move us to action.

Hume's acceptance in practice, for all his theoretical doubts, of the law of universal causation, is shown by his contention that our actions are caused by our passions as much, and as comprehensively, as natural events are by natural causes. That rules out 'liberty of indifference'. But the non-existence of unmotivated action is hardly a cause of concern. We often feel free in action and that is because we sometimes act without coercion or constraint: that is to say, in accordance with our desires. That is the kind of freedom that should concern us, for we can only be sensibly held responsible for actions that we have caused. Only they are going to be amenable to the sanctions of praise and blame, reward and punishment.

Hume proclaims the inertness of reason in his notorious pronouncement 'reason is and ought only to be the slave of the passions'. 'Ought only to be' is an irrelevant rhetorical flourish. So is 'slave', which should be 'serves instrumentally for the satisfaction of' and so is 'passion' in the sense in which we understand the word now. Moral convictions move us to action; reason alone cannot do so; therefore, moral convictions are not the product of reason. He offers a number of other rather elaborate and not very persuasive arguments for the conclusion. But he has a significant argument to show that the morality of an action is not a matter of fact. Take any action agreed to be vicious; examine it as hard as you can. You will never find vice in it. Much the same point is made in his contention that the passage from *is* to *ought*, everywhere to be found in moral discourse, should be explained or justified.

The source of morality in the passions is sympathy, the natural inclination to be pleased by the happiness, pained by the suffering, of others. That explains, associatively, the natural impulse of benevolence. Self-interest is natural or instinctive too, but it is not our exclusive form of motivation. Sympathy underlies the practice of disinterested contemplation of people's actions and characters. When the result of such contemplation is pleasant, it is moral approval; when unpleasant, disapproval. What is it about people's characters and actions that causes these emotional reactions (which, being emotions, are neither true nor false)? Hume's answer is that we react approvingly to what is useful or agreeable to the agent or others. But qualities useful or agreeable to the agent seem to be natural rather than moral virtues, gifts of character, like prudence or courage, rather than virtues strictly so called. Hume is not constrained by this over-inclusive formula. For the most part he explains the virtues by their contribution to the utility of society in general.

It is quite a short step from this position – but it is one that Hume does not take – to say that moral approval is not just *explained* by the utility of what it is bestowed on, but *implies* and is *justified* by the utility of what is approved. That would leave room – as Hume does not – for the correction of approvals as mistaken if they are based on false judgements of utility. He does not appear to doubt that utility, the 'good of society', is a straightforward matter of fact. That, of course, is the position of the utilitarians proper, Bentham above all, and, with qualifications, John Stuart Mill.

Hume recognizes that our natural instinct of benevolence, although an independent principle of action alongside self-interest, does not reach all that far and tends to prevail only in our dealings with those who are close to us. But, beside the natural virtue of benevolence, there is also the artificial virtue of justice. In human society we depend crucially on each other, much more than other, more self-reliant animals. But by co-operation we can increase our strength, by division of labour our skill and by mutual aid our security from misfortune. To establish these desirable arrangements we set up such institutions as promise-keeping, property and the state.

The duties of respect for property, fidelity and allegiance yield beneficial consequences only if they are generally adhered to. A single act of benevolence can do good on its own, but it is futile to respect property or obey a state that no one else respects or obeys. Hume on the whole identifies justice with respect for property. The scarcity of goods in relation to the strength of people's desire for them leads to conflict. Settled rules for the acquisition, possession and transfer of property are necessary for social peace. The rules of justice are useful only as a system, so the rules should be adhered to even where their application produces an exceptional bad result.

Justice and the other artificial virtues have no direct support from the passions. We all have a strong self-interested motive for general respect for them. That becomes moralized by the transfer of self-interested approval of them to a distinterested, moral approval of them as beneficial to society, an effect of sympathy.

Hume's treatment of allegiance, the duty to obey the state and abide by its laws, deserves separate consideration.

I shall first prove from experience, that our actions have a constant union with our motives, tempers, and circumstances, before I consider the inferences we draw from it.

To this end a very slight and general view of the common course of human affairs will be sufficient. There is no light, in which we can take them, that does not confirm this principle. Whether we consider mankind according to the difference of sexes, ages, governments, conditions, or methods of education; the same uniformity and regular operation of natural principles are discernible. Like causes still produce like effects; in the same manner as in the mutual action of the elements and powers of nature. (T 401)

After we have performed any action; though we confess we were influenced by particular views and motives; it is difficult for us to persuade ourselves we were governed by necessity, and that it was utterly impossible for us to have acted otherwise; the idea of necessity seeming to imply something of force, and violence, and constraint, of which we are not sensible. Few are capable of distinguishing betwixt the liberty of *spontaneity*, as it is called in the schools, and the liberty of *indifference*; betwixt that which is opposed to violence, and that which means a negation of necessity and causes. The first is even the most common sense of the word; and as it is only that species of liberty, which it concerns us to preserve, our thoughts have been principally turned towards it, and have almost universally confounded it with the other. (T 410)

Men are not blamed for such actions as they perform

ignorantly and casually, whatever may be the consequences. Why? but because the principles of these actions are only momentary, and terminate in them alone. Men are less blamed for such actions as they perform hastily or unpremeditately than for such as proceed from deliberation. For what reason? but because a hasty temper, though a constant cause or principle in the mind, operates only by intervals and infects not the whole character. Again, repentance wipes off every crime, if attended with a reformation of life and manners. How is this to be accounted for? not by asserting that actions render a person criminal merely as they are proofs of criminal principles in the mind; and when, by an alteration of these principles, they cease to be just proofs, they likewise cease to be criminal. But, except upon the doctrine of necessity, they never were just proofs, and consequently never were criminal. (E98–9)

Nothing is more usual in philosophy, and even in common life, than to talk of the combat of passion and reason, to give the preference to reason, and to assert that men are only so far virtuous as they conform themselves to its dictates. Every rational creature, it is said, is obliged to regulate his actions by reason; and if any other motive or principle challenge the direction of his conduct, he ought to oppose it, till it be entirely subdued, or at least brought to a conformity with that superior principle. On this method of thinking the greatest part of moral philosophy, ancient and modern, seems to be founded ... In order to show the fallacy of all this philosophy, I shall endeavour to prove *first*, that reason alone can never be a motive to any action of the will; and *secondly*, that it can never oppose passion in the direction of the will. (T 413)

It is obvious, that when we have the prospect of pain or pleasure from any object, we feel a consequent emotion of aversion or propensity, and are carried to avoid or embrace what will give us this uneasiness or satisfaction.

It is also obvious, that this emotion rests not here, but making us cast our view on every side, comprehends whatever objects are connected with its original one by the relation of cause and effect. Here then reasoning takes place to discover this relation; and according as our reasoning varies, our actions receive a subsequent variation. But it is evident in this case, that the impulse arises not from reason, but is only directed by it. It is from the prospect of pain or pleasure that the aversion or propensity arises towards any object; and these emotions extend themselves to the causes and effects of that object, as they are pointed out to us by reason and experience. It can never in the least concern us to know, that such objects are causes, and such others effects, if both the causes and effects be indifferent to us. When the objects themselves do not affect us, their connection can never give them any influence; and it is plain, that as reason is nothing but the discovery of this connection, it cannot be by its means that the objects are able to affect us.

Since reason alone can never produce any action, or give rise to volition, I infer, that the same faculty is as incapable of preventing volition, or of disputing the preference with any passion or emotion ... Thus it appears, that the principle, which opposes our passion, cannot be the same with reason, and is only called so in an improper sense. We speak not strictly and philosophically when we talk of the combat of passion and of reason. Reason is and ought only to be the slave of the passions, and can never pretend to any other office than to serve and obey them. (T 414–15)

If morality had naturally no influence on human passions and actions, it were in vain to take such pains to inculcate it; and nothing would be more fruitless than that multitude of rules and precepts, with which all moralists abound. Philosophy is commonly divided into *speculative* and *practical*; and as morality is always comprehended under the latter division, it is supposed to influence our passions and actions, and to go beyond

42

the calm and indolent judgements of the understanding. And this is confirmed by common experience, which informs us, that men are often governed by their duties, and are deterred from some actions by the opinion of injustice, and impelled to others by that of obligation.

Since morals, therefore, have an influence on the actions and affections, it follows, that they cannot be derived from reason; and that because reason alone, as we have already proved, can never have any such influence. Morals excite passions, and produce or prevent actions. Reason of itself is utterly impotent in this particular. The rules of morality, therefore, are not conclusions of our reason. (T 457)

But can there be any difficulty in proving, that vice and virtue are matters of fact, whose existence we can infer by reason? Take any action allowed to be vicious; wilful murder, for instance. Examine it in all lights, and see if you can find that matter of fact, or real existence, which you call *vice*. In whichever way you take it, you find only certain passions, motives, volitions, and thoughts. There is no other matter of fact in the case. The vice entirely escapes you, as long as you consider the object. You never can find it till you turn your reflection into your own breast, and find a sentiment of disapprobation, which arises in you, towards this action. Here is a matter of fact; but it is the object of feeling, not of reason. It lies in yourself, not in the object. So that when you pronounce any action or character to be vicious, you mean nothing, but that from the constitution of your nature you have a feeling or sentiment of blame from the contemplation of it. Vice and virtue, therefore, may be compared to sounds, colours, heat and cold, which, according to modern philosophy, are not qualities in objects, but perceptions in the mind; and this discovery in morals, like that other in physics, is to be regarded as a considerable advancement of the speculative sciences; though, like that too, it has little or no influence on practice. Nothing can be more real, or concern us more, than our own sentiments of pleasure and uneasiness;

and if these be favourable to virtue, and unfavourable to vice, no more can be requisite to the regulation of our conduct and behaviour.

I cannot forbear adding to these reasonings an observation, which may, perhaps, be found of some importance. In every system of morality, which I have hitherto met with, I have always remarked, that the author proceeds for some time in the ordinary way of reasoning, and establishes the being of a God, or makes observations concerning human affairs; when of a sudden I am surprised to find, that instead of the usual copulations of propositions, *is* and *is not*, I meet with no proposition that is not connected with an *ought*, or an *ought not*. The change is imperceptible; but is, however, of the last consequence. For as this ought, or ought not, expresses some new relation, or affirmation, it is necessary that it should be observed and explained; and at the same time that a reason should be given, for what seems altogether inconceivable, how this new relation can be a deduction from others, which are entirely different from it. (T 468–9)

We may observe, that all the circumstances requisite for its [sympathy's] operation are found in most of the virtues; which have, for the most part, a tendency to the good of society, or to that of the person possessed of them. If we compare all these circumstances, we shall not doubt, that sympathy is the chief source of moral distinctions; especially when we reflect, that no objection can be raised against this hypothesis in one case, which will not extend to all cases. Justice is certainly approved of for no other reason, than because it has a tendency to the public good; and the public good is indifferent to us, except so far as sympathy interests us in it. We may presume the like with regard to all the other virtues, which have a like tendency to the public good. They must derive all their merit from our sympathy with those, who reap any advantage from them; as the virtues, which have a tendency to the good of the person possessed of them, derive their merit from our sympathy with him. (T 618)

The only difference betwixt the natural virtues and justice lies in this, that the good, which results from the former, arises from every single act, and is the object of some natural passion; whereas a single act of justice, considered in itself, may often be contrary to the public good; and it is only the concurrence of mankind, in a general scheme or system of action, which is advantageous. When I relieve persons in distress, my natural humanity is my motive; and so far as my succour extends, so have I promoted the happiness of my fellow-creatures. But if we examine all the questions, that come before any tribunal of justice, we shall find, that, considering each case apart, it would as often be an instance of humanity to decide contrary to the laws of justice as conformable to them. Judges take from a poor man to give to a rich; they bestow on the dissolute the labour of the industrious; and put into the hands of the vicious the means of harming both themselves and others. The whole scheme, however, of law and justice is advantageous to the society; and it was with a view to this advantage, that men by their arbitrary conventions, established it. After it is once established by these conventions, it is *naturally* attended with a strong sentiment of morals; which can proceed from nothing but our sympathy with the interests of society. We need no other explication of that esteem, which attends such of the natural virtues as have a tendency to the public good. (T 579–80)

To avoid giving offence, I must here observe, that when I deny justice to be natural virtue, I make use of the word *natural*, only as opposed to *artificial*. In another sense of the word; as no principle of the human mind is more natural than a sense of virtue; so no virtue is more natural than justice. Mankind is an inventive species; and where an invention is obvious and absolutely necessary, it may as properly be said to be natural as anything that proceeds immediately from original principles, without the intervention of thought or reflection. Though the rules of justice be *artificial*, they are not *arbitrary*. Nor is the expression improper to call them *Laws of Nature*, if by natural we understand what is common to any species, or even if we confine it to mean what is inseparable from the species. (T 484)

Upon the whole, then, we are to consider this distinction betwixt justice and injustice, as having two different foundations, viz. that of *interest*, when men observe, that it is impossible to live in society without restraining themselves by certain rule, and that of *morality*, when this interest is once observed, and men receive a pleasure from the view of such actions as tend to the peace of society, and an uneasiness from such as are contrary to it. It is the voluntary convention and artifice of men, which makes the first interest take place; and therefore those laws of justice are so far to be considered as *artificial*. After that interest is once established and acknowledged, the sense of morality in the observance of these rules follows *naturally* and of itself; though it is certain, that it is augmented by a new *artifice*, and that the public instructions of politicians, and the private education of parents, contribute to the giving us a sense of honour and duty in the strict regulation of our actions with regard to the properties of others. (T 533–4)

POLITICS

Hume was interested in the politics of his own time in a fairly detached way as well as in the large generalities of political theory. His main achievement in the second field was his exemplary demolition of the contract theory of government. In opposition to theories of passive obedience and divine right, Hobbes and Locke, in their very different ways, contended that the duty to obey the government was contractual. The obedience promised was not unconditional (it was very nearly so in Hobbes, hardly at all in Locke).

Hume's argument against the contract theory was set out at some length in the second part of book III of the *Treatise* and repeated in a condensed and strengthened form in his easy 'Of the original contract'. No one believes they have promised to obey the government. Locke's view that the consent is 'tacit' is undermined by the fact that people born in a society have no more choice about leaving it than a shanghaied sailor has of evading the captain's orders by jumping into the sea. Nearly all existing governments originated in conquest or usurpation, although it may be that the first societies installed rulers, who would be war chiefs, by agreement.

His decisive objection is that, if the answer to the question 'why obey the government?' is 'I have promised to do so', the question then arises 'why keep promises?'. The answer to that is that promise-keeping serves the general interest of society. But that answer can also be given to the question about obeying the government. To answer that obedience is based on a promise is to make an 'unnecessary circuit'. Promise-keeping and allegiance are in the same position, along with respect for property. All of them are justified, as artificial, or systematic virtues, by the contribution their general observance makes to the well-being of everyone. From this utilitarian principle it follows that withdrawal of allegiance or rebellion are justified if the government is either too weak to provide protection and security – its defining function – or so oppressive that everyone would be better off without it. But Hume was no revolutionary and cautions very strongly against it.

Hume is not all that much of a liberal, certainly not in a declamatory way. 'Liberty is the perfection of civil society,' he says, 'but still authority must be acknowledged as essential to its very existence.' He is not any sort of democrat, thinking that an educated élite, in whom the calm passions predominate, should rule over the ignorant and thoughtless. His sceptically or rationally conservative views permeated the six volumes of his *History of England*, the first reasonably impartial history of England, which caused outrage to doctrinaire Whiggism by its animus against the irrational frenzy of the Puritans and of the Protestant reformers from whom they derived, was sympathetic to the plight of Charles I and not unsympathetic to Archbishop Laud. Charles I, he thought, was not wicked but incompetent in claiming prerogative rights to which he had a perfectly good title, without ensuring that he had the force to push his claims through.

> It cannot be denied, that all government is at first, founded on a contract, and that the most ancient rude combinations of mankind were formed chiefly by that principle. (Ess 454).

> Almost all the governments which exist at present, or of which their remains any record in story, have been founded originally, either on usurpation or conquest, or both, without any pretence of a fair consent or voluntary subjection of the people. (Ess 457)

> What necessity, therefore, is there to found the duty of *allegiance*, or obedience to magistrates, on that of *fidelity*, or a regard to promises, and to suppose that it is the consent of each individual which subjects him to government, when it appears that both allegiance and fidelity stand precisely on the same foundation, and are both submitted to by mankind, on account of the

apparent interests and necessities of human society? We are bound to obey our sovereign, it is said, because we have given a tacit promise to that purpose. But why are we bound to obey our promise? It must here be asserted that the commerce and intercourse of mankind, which are of such mighty advantage, can have no security where men pay no regard to their engagements. In like manner may it be said that men could not live at all in society, at least in a civilised society, without laws, and magistrates, and judges to prevent the encroachments of the strong upon the weak, of the violent upon the just and equitable. The obligation to allegiance being of like force and authority with the obligation to fidelity, we gain nothing by resolving the one into the other. The general interests or necessities of society are sufficient to establish both.

If the reason be asked of that obedience which we are bound to pay to government, I readily answer, *Because society could not otherwise subsist*; and this answer is clear and intelligible to all mankind. Your answer is, *Because we should keep our word*. But besides that nobody, till trained in a philosophical system, can either comprehend or relish this answer; besides this, say, you find yourself embarrassed when it is asked, *Why we are bound to keep our word?* Nor can you give any answer but what would immediately, without any circuit, have accounted for our obligation to allegiance. (Ess 468–9)

I perceive, that a promise arises entirely from human conventions, and is invented with a view to a certain interest. I seek, therefore, some such interest more immediately connected with government, and which may be at once the original motive to its institution and the source of our obedience to it. This interest I find to consist in the security and protection, which we enjoy in political society, and which we can never attain, when perfectly free and independent. As interest, therefore, is the immediate sanction of government, the one can have no longer being than the other; and whenever the civil magistrate carries his oppression so far as to render his authority perfectly intolerable, we are no longer bound to submit to it. The cause ceases; the effect must cease also. (T 550–1)

Where the public good evidently does not demand a change; it is certain, that the concurrence of all those titles, *original contract, long possession, present possession, succession*, and *positive laws*, forms the strongest title to sovereignty and is justly regarded as sacred and inviolable. (T 562)

In all governments, there is a perpetual intestine struggle, open or secret, between Authority and Liberty; and neither of them can ever absolutely prevail in the contest. A great sacrifice of liberty must necessarily be made in every government: yet even the authority, which confines liberty, can never, and perhaps ought never, in any constitition, to become quite entire and uncontrollable. The sultan is master of the life and fortune of any individual; but will not be permitted to impose new taxes on his subjects: a French monarch can impose taxes at pleasure; but would find it dangerous to attempt the lives and fortunes of individuals. Religion, also, in most countries, is commonly found to be a very intractable principle; and other principles or prejudices frequently resist all the authority of the civil magistrate; whose power, being founded upon opinion, can never subvert other opinions equally rooted with that of his title to dominion. The government, which, in common appellation, receives the appellation of free, is that which admits of a partition of power among several members, whose untitled authority is no less, or is commonly greater, than that of any monarch; but who, in the usual course of administration, must act by general and equal laws, that are previously known to all the members, and to all their subjects. In this sense, it must be owned, that liberty is the perfection of civil society; but still authority must be acknowledged essential to its very existence: and in those contests which so often take place between the one and the other, the latter may, on that account, challenge the preference. Unless perhaps one may say (and it may be said with some reason) that a circumstance, which is essential to the existence of civil society, must always support itself, and needs to be guarded with less jealousy, than one which contributes to its perfection, which the indolence of men is so apt to neglect, or their ignorance to overlook. (Ess 38–9)

RELIGION

Hume's writings on religion are as brilliant as anything he produced, and it seems reasonable to suppose that they are a large part of the practical point (which was never far from his thoughts) of his more theoretical inquiries. The least substantial, but by no means least entertaining, is *The Natural History of Religion*. Its main theme is the causes and consequences of the religious development of mankind from polytheism to monotheism. That there has been such a development is shown, he believes, by the polytheism of contemporary savages, whom our remote, primitive ancestors must have resembled. They were impelled into belief in gods by particular fearful or calamitous events, not by any sophisticated reflection on the origins of the universe as an ordered whole. A special concern to flatter and promote one god among the rest gave rise to monotheism. It is less tolerant than its savage predecessor. Another moral deficiency of monotheism is its preference for such 'monkish virtues' as humility as opposed to the courage and self-reliance of our ancestors. Belief in a god or gods is not natural like belief in an external world, since there are races in which it is not to be found.

The Dialogues on Natural Religion, which Hume prudently kept back from publication until after his death, is perhaps the most witty and scintillating of his works. It is certainly the most ironical, so that some readers have sought to identify the author, not with the most sceptical of the participants, Philo, but with the devout, but not fanatical, Cleanthes, who is the mouthpiece of Bishop Butler.

The principal target of the *Dialogues* is the argument from design, that well-loved intellectual device of the eighteenth century, which infers the existence of God from evidence of order and of the adaptation of means to ends in nature. Hume takes the argument to pieces with the utmost perseverance. The analogy between man and his productions on the one hand and God and nature on the other has a number of crippling defects. We have seen many men putting up buildings, but we have no direct access to gods putting up natures. It is wrong to ascribe perfections like unlimited power, wisdom and goodness to the hypothetical cause of something so suffused with imperfections as the natural world. Is it not, anyway, quite as much like a vegetable growth as it is like a mechanical contrivance? Perhaps, if of divine workmanship at all, it is the work of several gods, or of a young one or an old one. Whatever qualities his production justifies us in ascribing to the author of nature, they can have no bearing on our conduct. Never has such a large, widely believed and intellectually respectable doctrine been so devastatingly and so stylishly reduced to rubble.

Hume repels the claims of revelation, as contrasted with reason, in his essay on miracles in the first *Enquiry*. The central argument is concise but very hard to answer. Confronted by testimony to a supposed miracle, Hume says, we should ask whether it is even more of a miracle that the testimony should be false. Since the alleged miracles of the New Testament, observed by uneducated men with an emotional interest in their acceptance, have passed on to us through a long chain of limitedly reliable intermediaries, it is not in the least miraculous that the reports of them should be mistaken.

It appears to me, that, if we consider the improvement of human society, from rude beginnings to a state of greater perfection, polytheism or idolatry was, and necessarily must have been, the first and most ancient religion of mankind.

Polytheism or idolatrous worship, being founded entirely in vulgar traditions, is liable to this great inconvenience, that any practice or opinion, however barbarous or corrupted, may be authorized by it; and full scope is given, for knavery to impose on credulity, till morals and humanity be expelled from the religious systems of mankind. At the same time, idolatry is attended with this evident advantage, that, by limiting the powers and functions of its deities, it naturally admits the gods of other sects and nations to a share of divinity, and renders all the various deities, as well as rites, ceremonies, or traditions, compatible with each other. Theism is opposite in both its advantages and disadvantages. As that system supposes one sole deity, the perfection of reason and goodness, it should, if justly prosecuted, banish everything frivolous, unreasonable, or inhuman from religious worship, and set before men the most illustrious example, as well as the most commanding motives, of justice and benevolence. These mighty advantages are not indeed over-balanced (for that is not possible), but somewhat diminished, by inconveniences, which arise from the vices and prejudices of mankind. While one sole object of devotion is acknowledged, the worship of other deities is regarded as absurd and impious. Nay, this unity of object seems naturally to require the unity of faith and ceremonies, and furnishes designing men with a pretence for representing their adversaries as profane, and the objects of divine as well as human vengeance. For as each sect is positive that its own faith and worship are entirely acceptable to the deity, and as no one can conceive, that the same being should be pleased with different and opposite rites and principles; the several sects fall naturally into animosity, and mutually discharge on each other that sacred zeal and rancour, the most furious and implacable of all human passions. (N60)

There is an evident absurdity in pretending to demonstrate a matter of fact, or to prove it by any arguments *a priori*. Nothing is demonstrable, unless the contrary implies a contradiction. Whatever we conceive as existent, we can also conceive as non-existent. There is no being, therefore, whose non-existence implies a contradiction. Consequently, there is no being, whose existence is demonstrable. I propose this argument as entirely decisive, and am willing to rest the whole controversy on it. (D 232–3)

You, then, who are my accusers, have acknowledged, that the chief or sole argument for a divine existence (which I never questioned) is derived from the order of nature; where there appear such marks of intelligence and design, that you think it extravagant to assign for its cause, either, chance, or the blind and unguided force of matter . . .

When we infer any particular cause from an effect, we must proportion the one to the other, and can never be allowed to the cause any qualities, but what are exactly sufficient to produce the effect. A body of ten ounces raised in any scale may serve as a proof, that the counter-balancing weight exceeds ten ounces; but can never afford a reason that it exceeds a hundred. If the cause, assigned for any effect, be not sufficient to produce it, we must either reject that cause, or add to it such qualities as will give it a just proportion to the effect. But if we ascribe to it farther qualities, or affirm it capable of producing other effects, we can only indulge the licence of conjecture, and arbitrarily suppose the existence of qualities and energies, without reason or authority. (E 135–6)

I much doubt whether it be possible for a cause to be known only by its effect (as you have all along supposed) or to be of so singular and particular a nature as to have no parallel and no similarity with any other cause or object, that has ever fallen under our observation. It is only when two *species* of objects are found to be constantly conjoined, that we can infer the one from the other; and were an effect presented, which was entirely singular, and could not be comprehended under any known *species*, I do not see, that we could form any conjecture or inference at all concerning its cause. If experience and observation and analogy be, indeed, the only guides which we can reasonably follow in inferences of this nature; both the effect and cause must bear a similarity and resemblance to other effects and causes, which we know, and which we have found, in many instances, to be conjoined with each other. (E 148)

This contrariety of evidence, in the present case [miracles], may be derived from several different causes; from the opposition of contrary testimony; from the character or number of the witnesses; from the manner of their delivering their testimony; or from the union of all these circumstances. We entertain a suspicion concerning any matter of fact, when the witnesses contradict each other; when they are but few or of a doubtful character; when they have an interest in what they affirm; when they deliver their testimony with hesitation, or, on the contrary, with too violent asseverations. There are many other particulars of the same kind, which may diminish or destroy the force of any argument, derived from human testimony. (Ess 522–3)

Let us suppose, that the fact which they affirm, instead of being only marvellous, is really miraculous; and suppose also, that the testimony considered apart and in itself, amounts to an entire proof; in that case, there is proof against proof, of which the strongest must prevail, but still with a diminution of its force, in proportion to that of its antagonist.

A miracle is a violation of the laws of nature; and as a firm and unalterable experience has established these laws, the proof against a miracle, from the very nature of the fact, is as entire as any argument from experience can possibly be imagined. (Ess524)

Nothing is esteemed a miracle if it ever happen in the common course of nature. It is no miracle that a man, seemingly in good health, should die on a sudden; because such a kind of death, though more unusual than any other, has yet been frequently observed to happen. But it is a miracle, that a dead man should come to life: because that has never been observed in any age or country. There must, therefore, be a uniform experience against every miraculous event, otherwise the event would not merit that appellation. And as a uniform experience amounts to a proof, there is here a direct and full *proof*, from the nature of the fact, against the existence of any miracle; nor can such a proof be destroyed, or the miracle rendered credible, but by an opposite proof which is superior.

The plain consequence is (and it is a general maxim worthy of our attention), 'That no testimony is sufficient to establish a miracle, unless the testimony be of such a kind, that its falsehood would be more miraculous, than the fact, which it endeavours to establish; and even in that case there is a mutual destruction of arguments, and the superior only gives us an assurance suitable to that degree of force, which remains, after deducting the inferior'. When anyone tells me, that he saw a dead man restored to life, I immediately consider with myself, whether it be more probable, that this person should either deceive or be deceived, or that the fact, which he relates, should really have happened. I weigh the one miracle against the other; and according to the superiority, which I discover, I pronounce my decision, and always reject the greater miracle. If the falsehood of his testimony would be more miraculous, than the event which he relates; then, and not till then, can he pretend to command my belief and opinion. (Ess 525–6).

Upon the whole, we may conclude, that the *Christian Religion* not only was at first attended with miracles, but even at this day cannot be believed by any reasonable person without one. (Ess 544)

EPILOGUE

In a short survey like this there is no room to do more than mention two more fields in which Hume was active: economics and aesthetics. Several of his essays are on economic subjects. In his powerful defence of free trade and in his refutation of mercantilist superstitions about retained gold and silver as a measure of a country's wealth, he anticipated, and perhaps influenced, his devoted friend Adam Smith, whose *Wealth of Nations* came out in the year of Hume's death, just in time for him to read it.

His views on 'taste' are what one might suspect from his account of morality. Beauty is not an intrinsic property of things, but is projected on to them by disinterested contemplators who find their 'form and disposition' pleasing. Association leads us from such direct responses to others, which take account of the utility of things. A tapered column pleases, since its broader base suggests greater strength and solidity. He tries with great ingenuity to answer the question: why does tragedy give us pleasure?

Hume was a wonderful man. He combined two pairs of qualities that have a certain affinity, but are quite often not found together. On the cognitive side, he was both supremely intelligent and extraordinarily clever, the exclusive gifts, one might suggest, of Aristotle and Jean Cocteau. In the domain of character and conduct, he was both morally virtuous (Adam Smith thought him the most perfectly virtuous man he had ever encountered) and inexhaustibly good-natured and sociable (the respective characteristics of Johnson and Boswell). He is at once the most admirable and the most lovable of philosophers, except in the judgement of pedants and prigs. He is also, for all his portly frame, red face and strong Scottish accent, the least ridiculous.

In his own time he was respected for his *History*, but his philosophy was ignored and his views about religion were regarded with horror. Kant claimed to have been woken from dogmatic slumber by reading him, but Hume would have acknowledged no responsibility for the result. Bentham was also dazzled, but more straightforwardly, even if he drew socially radical consequences from Hume's principles. Hume was not solemn enough to appeal to John Stuart Mill, whose theory of knowledge is, all the same, a kind of domestication of Hume. Russell, as mischievous and joke-loving as Hume, saw his own philosophy as a combination of Hume with modern logic. Wherever analytic philosophy is alive, as it still is in quite a number of places, Hume, more than any other great philosopher of the past, is still a force to reckon with.